J
634
Jo

Johnson, Sylvia A

Apple trees

DATE DUE

JE 18 '86			
NO 19 '87			
10/20/95			
MAY 06 '86			
MAR 21 '97			
SE 07 '99			
MY 13 '02			
MR 21'06			
MY 28 '6			
SE 28 '22			

APPLE TREES

by Sylvia A. Johnson

Photographs by Hiroo Koike

A Lerner Natural Science Book

Lerner Publications Company ▪ Minneapolis

Sylvia A. Johnson, Series Editor

Translation of original text by Chaim Uri

Additional research by Jane Dallinger

The publisher wishes to thank Chuck St. John and the Washington State Apple Commission for their assistance in the preparation of this book.

Additional photographs courtesy of: pp. 15, 37, 39, 44, Washington State Apple Commission; pp. 36, 38, 40, 42, International Apple Institute; p. 41, New York State Agricultural Experiment Station, Cornell University.

The glossary on page 46 gives definitions and pronunciations of words shown in **bold type** in the text.

LIBRARY OF CONGRESS CATALOGING IN PUBLICATION DATA

Johnson, Sylvia A.
  Apple trees.

  (A Lerner natural science book)
  Adaptation of: Ringo, kudamono no himitsu / by Hiroo Koike.
  Includes index.
  Summary: Discusses the growth and cultivation of apple trees and the development, harvesting, and storage of apples.
  1. Apple—Juvenile literature. 2. Fruit—Juvenile literature. 3. Fruit trees—Juvenile literature. [1. Apple. 2. Fruit. 3. Fruit trees] I. Koike, Hiroo, ill. II. Koike, Hiroo. Ringo, kudamono no himitsu. III. Title. IV. Series.
SB363.J65 1983   634'.11   83-16230
ISBN 0-8225-1479-6

This edition first published 1983 by Lerner Publications Company.
Text copyright © 1983 by Lerner Publications Company.
Photographs copyright © 1976 by Hiroo Koike.
Text adapted from APPLE TREES copyright © 1976 by Hiroo Koike.
English language rights arranged by Kurita-Bando Literary Agency for Akane Shobo Publishers, Tokyo, Japan.

International Standard Book Number: 0-8225-1479-6
Library of Congress Catalog Card Number: 83-16230

   2   3   4   5   6   7   8   9   10   90   89   88   87   86   85   84

There are many different kinds of fruit trees grown all over the world, but apple trees are very special. In spring, their branches are covered with sweet-smelling blossoms of pink and white. During the warm months of summer, the trees are thick with glossy green leaves and tiny developing apples. When autumn comes with its cool winds, the branches bend under the weight of the ripe fruit.

This book describes the life of an apple tree in all the seasons of the year and explains the fascinating natural process that produces the tree's crisp, delicious fruit.

When dandelions bloom in spring, the first green leaves
appear on apple trees.

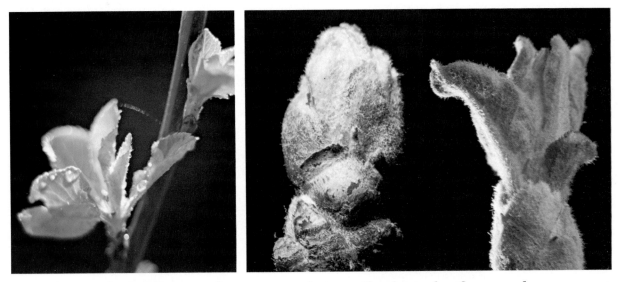

Left: Bright new leaves growing on the branch of an apple tree. *Right:* Flower buds gradually open after the leaves have appeared on the tree.

Fruit trees that produce oranges or grapefruits grow best in warm climates where temperatures are mild all year round. Apple trees are most at home in areas with cold winters. During the winter months, the trees rest and prepare for the growing season that is to come. Their branches look bare, but on the tips of their twigs are the **buds** that will develop into new leaves and flowers.

When the arrival of spring brings warmer temperatures and longer days, an apple tree comes to life. Its leaf buds begin to swell and to break through their protective coverings. Soon the first green leaves appear on the bare branches of the tree.

7

Covered with fresh young leaves, these apple trees will soon bloom with pink and white flowers.

Left: **Each of these flower buds is enclosed in five green sepals.** *Right:* **The sepals separate to reveal the pink apple flowers inside.**

At the same time that the new leaves are developing, the flower buds are beginning to swell with life. On fruit trees like the cherry and the peach, the flowers appear first, but apple flowers do not open until the tree is covered with leaves.

Apple flowers grow at the ends of twigs, usually in clusters of five. In the early stage of its development, a flower bud is surrounded and enclosed by five soft green **sepals**. These pointed, leaf-like structures make up the apple flower's calyx. The word **calyx** means "cup." As the flower bud grows larger, the sepals separate to form a kind of cup in which the opened flower will rest.

As the spring days become longer and warmer, the apple blossoms spread their petals and fill the tree with fragrant beauty. The flowers on most kinds of apple trees are pale pink when they first appear but become white when they are fully developed. Some apple trees, however, have deep pink or even purplish blossoms. The pictures on these two pages show a few of these varied and beautiful flowers.

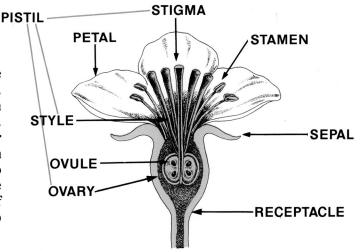

This drawing shows the parts of an apple flower. The pistil, the female organ of the flower, is compound. It is made up of five slender stalks, or styles, that join together at the bottom to form a single ovary with five compartments. At the tip of each style is a sticky knob called a stigma.

With their delicate colors and graceful petals, apple flowers look like fragile works of art. But they have a very practical function. Each flower is a tiny factory with parts that work together to produce the seeds from which new apple trees grow. As a by-product of this process, the flower will also produce a crisp red, green, or yellow apple.

An apple flower has the same basic parts as the flowers of other kinds of plants. In addition to its five green sepals, it has five pink or white petals. In the center of the flower are its reproductive parts—a large number of **stamens**, which produce male sperm cells, and one **pistil**, which produces female egg cells. It is through the union or **fertilization** of these sex cells that seeds and apples are created.

The sperm cells produced by the apple flower are contained in the powdery **pollen** manufactured in the **anthers**, the knobs on the ends of the stamens. Egg cells are produced in the **ovary**, the hollow chamber at the base of the pistil.

13

Inside the ovary are five little compartments, each containing two **ovules**. An ovule is made up of an egg cell plus all the other material needed to produce a seed. But the seed will begin to grow only when the egg cell is united with a sperm cell.

Although an apple flower produces both egg cells and sperm cells, the reproductive cells from a single flower usually do not join together to make seeds. Like many other kinds of plants, apple trees reproduce through the union of cells from two different trees. Since trees cannot move on their own, they need the help of an agent to make this union possible. Bees are the agents that help apple trees to reproduce by carrying sperm-bearing pollen from one tree to another.

Bees are so important to the development of apple trees that apple growers often move beehives into their orchards when the apple flowers are in bloom. The bees fly from flower to flower, seeking the sweet nectar that they need

The sweet fragrance of apple flowers attracts honeybees.

Apple growers often bring beehives into their orchards when the apple flowers are in bloom.

to produce honey. As a bee sucks nectar from a flower, its hairy body picks up the dust-like pollen from the anthers. When the bee moves on to another flower, some of the pollen rubs off on the **stigmas**, the sticky tips of the flower's pistil. Now the flower has been pollinated. The next step in the process is fertilization.

Fertilization takes place when pollen grains on the stigmas split open and send down long tubes into the pistil's ovary. Sperm cells move down the tubes and unite with the egg cells in the tiny ovules. When the egg cells have been fertilized, the ovules begin to develop into seeds.

Once fertilization has taken place, the petals of the apple flowers fade and fall off the tree (left). Their job of attracting bees and providing a landing platform for them is finished. Some of the other flower parts remain in place (above). The many stamens with their yellow anthers are still there, even though pollen is no longer being produced. Surrounded by the stamens, the five slender stalks of the pistil can still be seen.

Deep in the ovary, hidden by the green cup of the calyx, the real work of the flower is going on.

Opposite: In this enlarged photograph, you can see how the sepals pull together to form a tube around the stamens and other flower parts. *Right:* Developing young apples wet with dew.

As the seeds develop in the ovary, the five sepals of the calyx pull together until they form a kind of tube (opposite). This happens only when most of the ovules in the apple flower have been fertilized. The "standing-up" of the calyx is a sure sign that seeds are growing. It is also a sign that a tiny young apple will soon appear.

The apple can first be seen as a swelling at the base of the ovary, where the flower joins the stem. This part of the flower is called the **receptacle**. As the swelling of the receptacle gets bigger, it begins to take on the round shape of an apple. At the top of the little apple are the withered remains of the calyx, the stamens, and the pistil. These flower parts will remain on the apple as it continues to grow.

Inside the fuzzy green covering of the apple, other flower parts are developing into the core and white flesh of the mature fruit. Let's take a closer look at this remarkable development.

19

Apples and pears are closely related fruits and develop in the same way.

Because the apple is a fruit, its development follows a pattern common in the plant world. We usually use the word **fruit** to refer only to sweet, juicy plant foods like apples, peaches, or oranges. To a botanist—a scientist who studies plants—the word has a much wider meaning. It is used to describe the part of any flowering plant that encloses and protects the seeds.

The fruits of flowering plants like the grass that grows on our lawns are so small and inconspicuous that they are hard to see. Fruits that we eat, like apples or cucumbers (which is a fruit in the botanical sense), are larger and often contain fleshy plant tissue. What all these fruits have in common is that they have developed from flower ovaries and surrounding plant parts.

The apple and other familiar sweet fruits such as pears, peaches, and oranges develop from a single ovary. Botanists classify them as **simple fruits.** Strawberries and raspberries are **compound fruits** because they develop from several ovaries.

20

THE DEVELOPMENT OF AN APPLE FLOWER INTO AN APPLE

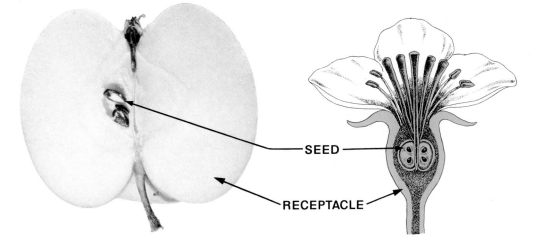

SEED

RECEPTACLE

The ovary of the apple flower, like that of most other flowers, is made up of several different layers or walls. It is the outer wall of the ovary, along with the tissue of the receptacle, that develops into the fleshy white part of the apple. The inner ovary wall becomes hard and papery. It forms the apple "core," which encloses the seeds. If you cut an apple in half crosswise, you will see that the core is divided into five sections, just like the flower ovary. (The photograph on page 26 shows these five sections.) Each section usually contains two seeds that developed from the two ovules.

Pears are closely related to apples and develop in the same way. Fruits with this kind of structure are known as **pomes** or core fruits. Several other types of simple fruits are shown on the next two pages.

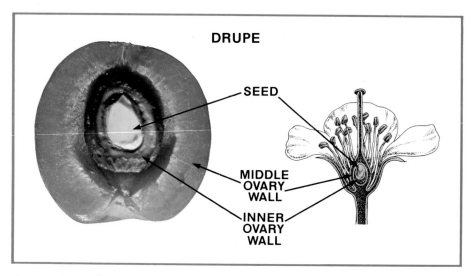

DRUPE

SEED

MIDDLE OVARY WALL

INNER OVARY WALL

An apricot develops from an ovary that contains a single seed. The seed is surrounded by a hard "stone" that grows from the inner ovary wall. The soft flesh of the fruit is produced by the middle layer of the ovary, while the outer layer forms the thin skin.

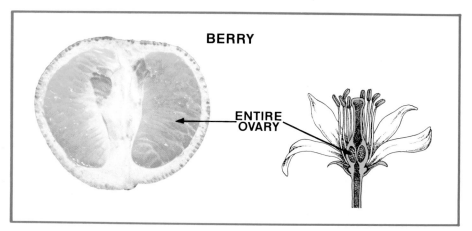

BERRY

ENTIRE OVARY

The ovary of an orange flower is divided into sections, each containing several seeds. All layers of the ovary develop into the juicy pulp surrounding the seeds in the fruit. A leathery rind forms on the outside of the pulp.

22

Grapes (right) are classified as berries because they have a pulpy flesh surrounding several seeds. Other fruits of this type include bananas, watermelons, tomatoes, grapefruits, and green peppers. Most of the fruits we call berries are not berries in the botanical sense but compound aggregate fruits.

Like the apricot, nectarines (above) and cherries (right) are drupes—fruits with a hard stone or pit surrounding a single seed. Peaches and plums also belong in the group.

Opposite: A young apple developing on the tree. *Right:* These apples have fallen off their trees because they did not get enough nourishment.

Like all fruits, an apple is nourished by its parent tree as it goes through the long, slow process of development. Using the energy of the bright summer sun, the tree's green leaves manufacture a form of sugar called **glucose**. The sugar is carried from the leaves to the fruit and the other parts of the tree. There it is used as food for growth or stored for future use in the form of starch.

About 50 or 60 leaves are needed to produce the food necessary for the growth of a single apple. If a tree bears a large number of apples, it will not be able to manufacture enough food for their continued development. Without adequate nourishment, some of the apples stop growing and fall off the tree. Apple growers call this the "June drop" since it usually takes place in the month of June. After the June drop, the apples remaining on the tree will receive enough nutrients to continue their growth.

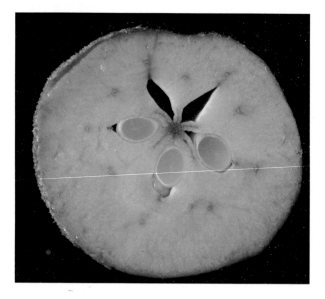

This apple is developing unevenly because not all of its ovules were fertilized and transformed into seeds. As you can see, two of the five seed chambers in the apple core are empty. Seeds contain a growth hormone that plays a part in the apple's development. Without this hormone, the flesh on one side of the apple cannot grow normally. The result is an apple with a lopsided shape.

As an apple grows, its cells divide and become larger. The picture on the left shows the small cells of a young apple beginning its development in June. You can see some of the hairs that grow on its skin (indicated by arrows). By August, the cells in the apple are much larger and not so closely packed together (middle). By September, the apple has almost completed its development. It contains very large cells with a lot of space between them (right). This space is filled with water, which makes up about 85 percent of an average apple.

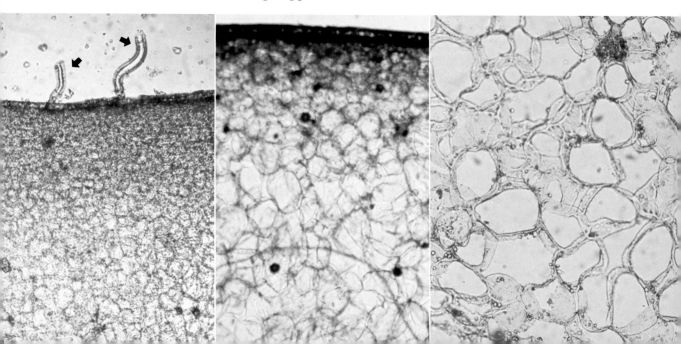

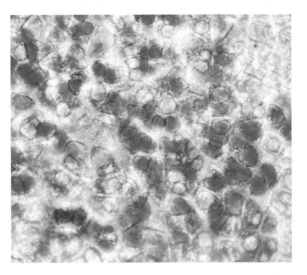

This enlarged picture shows how red pigment forms in the cells of an apple's skin.

During the warm months of summer, the apples on a tree grow larger and larger. By the time the apples have reached their full size, they no longer depend on the tree for nourishment. Instead they produce their own food by turning the starch stored in their flesh back into sugar. It is this process that makes a fully developed apple taste sweet.

The transformation of starch into sugar is also part of the process that makes a ripe apple turn red. The presence of sugar, plus the bright light of the sun, produces chemical reactions in the apple. These reactions cause the cells in the apple's skin to produce a red **pigment** called anthocyanin. Other pigments create the yellow colors in an apple's skin.

This change of color is a sign of ripeness in most apples, an indication that the fruit and the seeds are fully developed. Of course, some apples do not change color but remain green even when they are mature.

By September or October, the apples are hanging, ripe and sweet, from the branches of the trees. If they are not picked by humans and used as food, they will fall to the ground, where they will be eaten by birds, deer, and other animals. The seeds will be scattered, and some of them will eventually develop into new apple trees.

29

Left: A new bud begins its development while the leaves on the apple tree are green and fresh. *Right:* By the time that the leaves change color in the autumn, the bud is completely formed. It is covered with hair to protect it from the cold winter weather.

Producing seeds and the apples that enclose them is an apple tree's biggest job during the year, but it has another task to perform before it can shed its leaves and prepare for its winter rest. The tree must produce the buds from which next year's leaves and flowers will grow.

The buds begin to develop during the summer, while the apples are on the tree. By the time the apples are gone and the leaves have begun to turn yellow, the buds are completely formed. They are covered with a hairy coat that will help to protect them during the cold winter months that are to come.

After finishing the hard work of producing seeds and buds, the leaves of apple trees change color and fall to the ground.

The cold temperatures and heavy snows of winter do not harm the buds on the apple trees. Protected by their hairy coverings, they rest quietly, waiting for the coming of spring and a new season of flowering and growth.

An apple tree's seasonal cycle of growth and reproduction is the same as that of many other kinds of flowering plants. But most apple trees grown today do not follow a completely natural pattern of development. Their habits have been changed by thousands of years of human intervention.

Scientists believe that the apple tree was one of the earliest trees **domesticated** by the human race. Archaeologists have found evidence that people living in Europe in prehistoric times grew apples as food. By the time of the Roman Empire, many varieties of apples were cultivated throughout Europe.

All these cultivated apples were probably developed from a kind of wild crabapple that can still be found in some parts of the world. The fruit of a crabapple tree is usually hard and sour, but early people soon learned to grow trees that produced sweet, edible fruit. Today apple growers all over the world use similar methods to produce millions of apples that not only taste good but also have an attractive appearance. The simple natural process by which apple trees reproduce has become the basis of a very big business.

These large, perfectly shaped red apples are the product of the modern apple-growing industry.

Seeds are the reason why apple trees produce apples, but today very few apples grow on trees that have been raised from seeds.

Planting apple seeds is a very uncertain business. You can never be sure that you will get a tree like the tree from which the seeds came. This is because apple seeds are formed by the union of egg cells from one tree and sperm cells from many other trees that grow in the same area. Such cross-fertilization results in **hybrid** seeds with the combined characteristics of different parent trees. Trees grown from these seeds will usually produce apples with a similar blend of characteristics.

But most commercial growers want trees that bear a specific kind of apple, one that they know grows well in their area and that their customers will buy. In order to get the kind of apples they want, growers plant trees created by the technique of **grafting**.

SCION

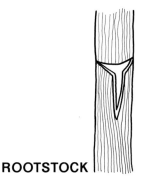

ROOTSTOCK

In bud grafting, a bud with a piece of bark attached is cut from one tree. The bud, or scion, is put into a T-shaped cut made in a second tree called the rootstock. The two pieces are bound together with string or tape.

Grafting is a method that uses parts of two existing trees to produce a new tree. A grafter takes a young tree and cuts it off close to the ground, leaving only part of the trunk. Then a bud is removed from a mature tree that bears the kind of apples the grafter wants to reproduce. The bud is forced into a cut made in the bark of the first tree. Eventually the two joined parts develop into a single tree.

The first tree, called the **rootstock**, provides the roots for the new tree, but the grafted bud, known as the **scion**, will determine the kind of apples that the tree will bear. For example, a scion taken from a tree that produces McIntosh apples will create a new tree that bears McIntoshes, no matter what kind of rootstock it is joined to.

By planting young trees created through grafting, growers can be sure that their orchards will produce just the variety of apples that they want to grow.

The McIntosh is a very popular apple in North America. Like many well-known varieties, it developed by chance, first appearing in the 1800s on the land of a Canadian farmer named McIntosh. The juicy, bright red McIntosh apple is usually eaten fresh rather than used for cooking.

When it comes to selecting a variety of apple, growers have a very wide choice. There are at least 7,500 varieties known today, and more are being developed each year. This great variety in apple types is possible because apple trees produce hybrid seeds so easily.

Some apple varieties originated accidentally, through the natural process of pollination and fertilization. Others were developed by scientists using controlled methods of breeding. Once a desirable new variety appears on a tree grown from seeds, it can be reproduced through grafting to create hundreds of new trees bearing the same kind of apple.

The pictures on these pages show a few of the apple varieties grown today.

Many new varieties of apples appear on the world market each year. The Granny Smith (right) is a bright green apple that is grown in Australia, South Africa, Chile, and other countries in the Southern Hemisphere. It keeps very well and is often shipped to North America and Europe. In recent years, growers in the United States have also begun producing Granny Smith apples.

With its oval shape, striped skin, and knobby bottom, the Red Delicious (left) is an apple with an unmistakable appearance. The most popular variety in the United States, it is also grown and eaten in many other parts of the world. A close runner-up in popularity is the Golden Delicious (right). Despite the similarity of their names, the two varieties are not related. Both developed by accident in the United States during the 1800s.

Growing any variety of apple on a large scale is a very complicated business. Apple growers must work hard to make sure that their trees produce healthy and attractive apples.

The long process of growing apples usually begins when a grower gets a supply of young grafted trees raised in a tree nursery. The little trees, no more than a year old, are planted in long rows about 20 feet (6 meters) apart. This spacing gives the trees room to grow and also allows the orchard owner to bring in the equipment needed to care for the trees.

A young apple tree must grow for several years before it starts producing apples. A few varieties have been developed that bear apples when they are only 3 years old, but most other kinds of trees must be 7 to 10 years old before they reach their reproductive stage.

An orchard of young trees

Irrigation is sometimes necessary to give apple trees the moisture they need to grow.

During these growing years, the grower carefully tends the apple trees, nourishing them with fertilizers and keeping an eye out for signs of disease. In areas where there is not enough rainfall, orchard owners use irrigation to make sure that their trees get enough moisture. Most of the orchards in the state of Washington, the leading apple producer in the United States, are watered throughout the growing season by sprinklers placed among the trees.

Finally, after years of loving care, the trees begin to produce apples. Then the grower's work really begins.

This truck is spraying insecticide on the apple trees in an orchard.

One of an apple grower's biggest jobs is protecting the apples from insects and disease. There are several kinds of insects that can cause a great deal of damage by boring holes in apples or attacking the young leaves in the spring. (The photographs on the opposite page show some of these insects.)

To get rid of such pests, growers spray the trees with **insecticides**, poisonous chemicals that kill the insects. But insecticides have to be used carefully, or they can kill helpful insects as well as harmful ones. Some growers try to use natural controls against insect pests, for example, by introducing natural enemies of the insects into an orchard.

The caterpillar (left) of the codling moth (right) can cause great destruction in an apple orchard. The female moth lays her eggs on the leaves of the trees. When the caterpillars hatch, they burrow into the apples and feed on their flesh.

The European red mite attacks apple trees by sucking the sap from new leaves in spring. Natural enemies such as ladybugs and other species of mites help growers in their battle against this insect pest.

The female apple fly (left) lays her eggs under the skin of a developing apple. After hatching from their eggs, apple fly maggots (right) make their home inside the apple for four to six weeks before going on to the next stage of their development.

Tall ladders are needed to reach apples on the top of a tree.

After protecting the apples through the long summer growing season, the grower must get ready for the busy autumn harvest. Some varieties of apples are ripe and ready for picking in August, but most kinds are not completely developed until September or October.

Commercially grown apples are usually picked by hand to keep them safe from bruises and other injuries. Pickers carefully twist the apples from the branches of the trees, putting them into canvas bags worn over their shoulders. They use tall ladders to reach the apples at the tops of the trees.

It is easier to pick apples from "dwarf" trees. Growers also like dwarf trees because they take up less room in an orchard and begin producing apples sooner than full-size trees.

Once the apples are off the tree, they are sorted into groups according to their size and condition. Apples that are small and not perfectly formed are often processed rather than sold fresh. Today most people want their apples to be large and beautiful as well as tasty.

Modern storage methods have made it possible to have fresh apples long after the autumn harvest. Growers put their apples into cold storage, at temperatures as low as 30 degrees Fahrenheit (−3 Celsius). The cold keeps the apples fresh by slowing down the natural process that causes withering and decay. A special storage technique slows down this process even more by decreasing the amount of oxygen in the air. This method makes it possible to have fresh apples available throughout the year.

Pruning is a wintertime job in an apple orchard.

Even after the autumn harvest is over and the apples are safely stored away, a grower's work is not done. During the winter months, the apple trees must be pruned. **Pruning** is a method of cutting and trimming the trees to increase their production of apples.

If allowed to grow naturally, an apple tree will become bushy and round in shape. The upper branches will grow thickly, shading the lower branches from the sun and reducing their ability to produce apples. In order to avoid this, a grower trims the tree into a kind of pyramid shape, with the upper branches shorter than the lower ones.

An apple tree is carefully pruned when it is young to make sure that it grows into the right shape. Additional pruning is done every winter during the tree's productive life.

Apple trees usually continue producing apples for about 40 or 50 years. Each year, the fragile blossoms appear in spring, and the fruit grows and ripens under the summer sun. Each year, the golden leaves fall in autumn, and the trees rest through the cold winter, preparing for the next season of growth.

The next time that you bite into a crisp, juicy apple, think about the marvellous natural process that created it and the many years of human effort that helped it to grow.

GLOSSARY

anthers—the knobs at the ends of the stamens where pollen is produced

buds—the parts of a plant that will develop into new flowers and leaves

calyx (KAY-licks)—a cup-shaped structure formed by a flower's sepals

compound fruits—fruits formed from flowers with more than one ovary

domesticated—tamed and raised by humans

fertilization—the union of a male sperm cell and a female egg cell

fruit—the part of a plant that encloses and protects the seeds

glucose (GLU-kose)—a form of sugar manufactured by plants during the process of **photosynthesis**

grafting—joining parts of two existing plants to form a new plant

hybrid (HI-brid) seeds—seeds produced by parent plants with different characteristics

insecticides (in-SEK-tih-sides)—chemicals and other poisonous substances used to kill insect pests

ovary (OH-vuh-ree)—the hollow chamber at the base of the pistil where seeds are formed

ovules (AHV-yuls)—tiny structures in a plant's ovary that contain female egg cells. After fertilization, ovules develop into seeds.

photosynthesis (fot-uh-SIN-thih-sis)—the process by which green plants use the energy of the sun to make food

pigment—material in plant and animal cells that produces color

pistil (PIS-t'l)—the female reproductive organ of a flower

pollen—a powdery substance produced by the anthers, containing male sperm cells

pomes (POHMS)—fleshy fruits with a hard core enclosing the seeds

pruning—trimming and cutting a plant to change its shape

receptacle (ree-SEP-tih-kuhl)—the part of a flower that is connected to the stalk

rootstock—the part of a grafted plant that provides the roots

scion (SI-uhn)—the part of a grafted plant that determines the kind of fruit the plant will bear

sepals (SEE-puhls)—the leaf-like structures that make up a flower's calyx

simple fruits—fruits formed from flowers with a single ovary

stamens (STAY-muhns)—the male reproductive organs of a flower

stigma—the sticky tip of a flower's pistil

INDEX

anthers, 13, 17
anthocyanin, 27

beehives, 15
bees, 14-15, 17
berries, 22
buds, 7, 9; formation of, 30;
    use of, in grafting, 35

calyx, 9, 17, 19
climate suitable for apple
    trees, 7
color, development of, 27
compound fruits, 20
core, 19, 21
crabapple, 33

Delicious apples, 37
domestication of apple trees,
    33
drupes, 22

egg cells, 13, 14

fertilization, 13, 15
flowers, 8, 13, 17; colors of,
    10; parts of, 13-14, 19
fruit, botanical meaning of,
    20

glucose, 25
grafting, 34-35, 36
Granny Smith apples, 37

harvesting apples, 42
hybrid seeds, 34

insecticides, 40
insect pests, 40-41
irrigation, 39

June drop, 25

leaves, 7, 8; role of, in
    producing food, 25
life span of apple tree, 45

McIntosh apples, 35, 36

nectar, 15

ovary, 13-14, 15, 17; develop-
    ment of, into fruit, 20-23
ovules, 14, 15, 19

pears, relation of, to apples,
    21
pigment, 27
pistil, 13, 15, 17, 19
planting apple trees, 38
pollen, 13, 14-15, 17
pollination, 15
pomes, 21
pruning, 45

receptacle, 19
reproduction, 13-15
rootstock, 35

scion, 35
seeds, 13, 29, 34; formation
    of, 15, 19
sepals, 9, 13
simple fruits, 20
sperm cells, 13, 14
stamens, 13, 17, 19
starch, 25, 27
stigmas, 15
storage of apples, 43
sugar, 25, 27

varieties of apples, 34, 35,
    36-37